OLIVER KNUSSEN

Horn Concerto

Op.28

(1994)

FABER *ff* MUSIC

Commissioned by Suntory Limited for the
Suntory International Program for Music Composition in 1994

The first performance was given by Barry Tuckwell with the Tokyo
Metropolitan Symphony Orchestra conducted by the composer
at Suntory Hall, Tokyo on 7 October 1994

The *Horn Concerto* is recorded by Barry Tuckwell with the London Sinfonietta
conducted by the composer on Deutsche Grammophon CD 449 572-2

© 1996 by Faber Music Ltd
First published in 1996 by Faber Music Ltd
3 Queen Square London WC1N 3AU
Music processed by Dennis Riley
Printed in England by Intype London
All rights reserved

ISBN 0-571-51667-X

To buy Faber Music publications or to find out about the full range of titles available
please contact your local music retailer or Faber Music sales enquiries:

Faber Music Limited, Burnt Mill, Elizabeth Way, Harlow, CM20 2HX England
Tel: +44 (0)1279 82 89 82   Fax: +44 (0)1279 82 89 83
sales@fabermusic.com   fabermusic.com

for Barry Tuckwell

ORCHESTRA

4 Flutes (3 and 4 = piccolos)
2 Oboes
Cor anglais
3 Clarinets in B♭ (3 = E♭ clarinet)
Bass clarinet
2 Bassoons
Contrabassoon

4 Horns in F
2 Trumpets in C
2 Tenor trombones

Timpani (2 players)
    4 drums each, placed left and right of the orchestra

Percussion (2 players)
    I Marimba, Triangle
    II 2 large Tam-tams, suspended Cymbal

Celesta

Harp

Strings (preferably 14-12-10-8-8)

N.B. The orchestral horns should be placed on the opposite side of the stage from the solo horn, so that if the soloist stands to the left of the conductor, the orchestral horns will sit to the rear right of the orchestra.

Duration approximately 13 minutes

*all remaining stands enter *div.*, *sul tasto*, but *without* mutes.

Fantastico (♩ = 92)
5
SOLO
a 2
3.
Fl.
Ob.
C. A.
Cl. (B♭)
Bs. Cl. (B♭)
Bsn.
Cbsn.
Hn. (F)
Tr.
Tbn.
Timp.
aperto
Mar.
Perc.
Cel.
Harp
G♭
E♭
table
SOLO HORN (F)
leggiero
poco
Fantastico (♩ = 92)
35
Vlns. I
unis., pizz.
div., arco
Vlns. II
pizz.
arco, sul tasto
Vas. div.
sul tasto
ord.
poco sfz
Vlc.
unis.
div.
Db.
5

Willow Cottage
25 August-30 September 1994
revised October 1995